Celebrate
Independence
Day

by Sally Lee

PEBBLE
a capstone imprint

First Facts are published by Pebble,
1710 Roe Crest Drive, North Mankato, Minnesota 56003
www.mycapstone.com

Library of Congress Cataloging-in-Publication Data
Library of Congress Cataloging-in-Publication data is available on the Library of Congress website.
ISBN 978-1-9771-0279-9 (library binding)
ISBN 978-1-9771-0534-9 (paperback)
ISBN 978-1-9771-0287-4 (eBook PDF)

Editorial Credits
Mandy Robbins, editor; Cynthia Della-Rovere, designer; Pam Mitsakos, media researcher;
Tori Abraham, production specialist

Photo Credits
Getty Images: Photographer's Choice/Ariel Skelley, Cover: iStockphoto/M_a_y_a, 16-17; Newscom:
akg-images, 10-11, Picture History, 7 (bottom right); North Wind Picture Archives: 7 (top left), 15;
Shutterstock: Bokeh Blur, Design Element, Dmytro Balkhovitin, 3, (bottom left), 20-21, Duda Vasillii,
Design Element, Everett Historical, 12-13, katjen, 4-5, Roberto Galan, 18-19, sharpner, 1 (bottom);
spatuletail, 8-9

Printed and bound in the United States of America.
PA49

Table of Contents

Happy Birthday, America!

Independence Day is the birthday of the United States of America. It celebrates the day the nation declared its independence from Great Britain. Americans celebrate it every year on July 4th.

independence—the state of being free from the control of other people or governments

The Fight for Independence

Before there were states, Americans lived in 13 *colonies*. They were governed by Great Britain's *Parliament* and King George III. When Great Britain needed money, it raised the colonists' *taxes*. The colonists thought this was unfair. They had no say in Parliament.

colony—an area of land ruled by a faraway country
Parliament—the law-making body of British government
tax—money that people or businesses must give to the government to pay for what the government does

A colonist named Daniel Dulany wrote this paper speaking out about the new taxes.

King George III

CONSIDERATIONS

James ON THE *Tilghman*

PROPRIETY

OF IMPOSING

TAXES

IN THE

British COLONIES,

For the Purpose of raising a REVENUE, by ACT OF PARLIAMENT.

By Mr Daniel Delaney

——Haud Totum Verba refignent
Quod latet arcanâ, non enarrabile, fibrâ.

North-America: Printed by a North-American.
MDCCLXV.

The colonists thought it was unfair that they had no say in British government. They *protested* the new laws and taxes. King George III ignored their complaints. He sent soldiers to the colonies to keep order. Many colonists thought it was time to form their own country.

protest—to say you think something is wrong and needs to be changed

During the Boston Tea Party, colonists protested the British tax on tea. They threw crates of British tea into the ocean.

Representatives from all 13 colonies met in 1776. They voted to break away from Great Britain. Thomas Jefferson used their ideas to write the *Declaration* of Independence. It was adopted on July 4, 1776.

representative—someone who is chosen to act or speak for others

declaration—an official statement or the document that contains it

Colonial leaders sign the Declaration of Independence.

It took more than words to win freedom. The colonists fought the British soldiers in the *Revolutionary* War (1775–1783). In the end the colonists won. They no longer lived in colonies. They lived in the United States of America.

Fact George Washington led the *Continental* army. He became America's first president.

revolution—an attempt to overthrow a government and replace it with a new system

Continental—relating to the 13 colonies that became the United States

The colonists fight the British during the Battle of Bunker Hill.

Let's Celebrate!

Philadelphia held the first Independence Day celebration on July 4, 1777. The day included speeches, music, and fireworks. Soon other towns began holding celebrations. *Congress* made Independence Day an official holiday in 1870.

Fact Philadelphia was the capital of the United States from 1790 to 1800.

Congress—the branch of a national government that makes laws

Independence Hall in Philadelphia

Independence Day is a giant birthday celebration. Schools, businesses, and government offices shut down. Cities have big parades with bands and floats. Neighborhoods have small parades. Kids decorate their bikes with red, white, and blue streamers. Friends and families have picnics.

Fact All U.S. major-league baseball teams wear red, white, and blue uniforms on Independence Day.

Some songs capture the spirit of Independence Day. Francis Scott Key wrote *The Star-Spangled Banner* in 1814. Today it is the U.S. national *anthem*. *America the Beautiful* and *God Bless America* are two other *patriotic* songs. Marching bands play songs such as these in parades.

anthem—a song of praise, often for one's country
patriotic—feeling or showing love and pride for one's country

18

John Philip Sousa

John Philip Sousa wrote 136 marches more than 100 years ago. He was known as the "March King." Sousa's *Stars and Stripes Forever* is America's national march.

Across the country, Independence Day ends with a bang. The night sky lights up as bright fireworks burst in the air. The pops and booms sound like the cannons used to win the country's freedom. It is a sparkling reminder of the nation's history.

True Meaning

Independence Day is more than flags, fireworks, and food. It is a day to remember those who created our country. It is also a day to thank members of the military who work to protect it.

Glossary

anthem (AN-thuhm)—a song of praise for one's country

colony (KAH-luh-nee)—land ruled by a faraway country

Congress (KAHNG-gruhs)—the branch of a national government that makes laws

Continental (KAHN-tuh-nen-tuhl)—relating to the 13 colonies that became the United States

declaration (dek-luh-RAY-shuhn)—an official statement or the document that contains it

independence (in-di-PEN-duhnss)—the state of being free from the control of other people or governments

Parliament (PAR-luh-muhnt)—the law-making body of British government

patriotic (pay-tree-OT-ik)—feeling or showing love and pride for one's country

protest (PRO-test)—to say you think something is wrong and needs to be changed

representative (rep-ri-ZEN-tuh-tiv)—someone who is chosen to act or speak for others

revolution (rev-uh-LOO-shun)—an attempt to overthrow a government and replace it with a new system

tax (TAKS)—money that people or businesses must give to the government to pay for what the government does

Read More

Mara, Wil. *If You Were a Kid During the American Revolution.* If You Were a Kid. New York: Children's Press, an imprint of Scholastic Inc., 2017.

Potter, Jonathan. *Why Do We Celebrate Independence Day?* Celebrating U.S. Holidays. New York: PowerKids Press, 2019.

Winter, Jonah. *The Founding Fathers!: Those Horse-Ridin', Fiddle-Playin', Book-Readin', Gun-Totin' Gentlemen Who Started America.* New York: Atheneum Books America, 2015.

Internet Sites

Use FactHound to find Internet sites related to this book.

Visit www.facthound.com

Just type in 9781977102799 and go.

Super-cool stuff!

Check out projects, games and lots more at
www.capstonekids.com

Critical Thinking Questions

1. Why is Independence Day called the birthday of the United States?

2. Why did the 13 colonies want to be free from Great Britain?

3. How do you celebrate Independence Day?

Index